Tired of jogging?
Bored with racketball?
Had it with health club bills?
Well, then **SKIP IT!**

SKIP TO A HEALTHY HEART

will teach you how to skip rope like a professional athlete in just 2 short weeks. Rope skipping is great exercise for your entire body and one of the best ways to keep your heart in shape.

Join the millions of people who have made
rope skipping a regular part of their
exercise program.

Whether you're 9 or 90 you can skip rope.
All you need is the rope to

SKIP TO A HEALTHY HEART

Skip To A Healthy Heart

Candace Lyle Hogan

Prince Paperbacks
Crown Publishers, Inc.
New York

Copyright © 1985 by Candace Lyle Hogan

A Prince Paperback Book

Published by Crown Publishers, Inc., One Park Avenue, New York, New York 10016 and simultaneously in Canada by General Publishing Company Limited

Manufactured in the United States of America

CROWN, PRINCE PAPERBACKS, and colophon are trademarks of Crown Publishers, Inc.

Library of Congress Cataloging in Publication Data

Hogan, Candace Lyle.
    Skip to a healthy heart.

    (Prince paperbacks)
    1. Health.   2. Rope skipping   3. Heart—Diseases—
Prevention.   I. Title.
RA781.H62   1985   613.7′1   85-5923
ISBN 0-517-55736-3 (pbk.)
10   9   8   7   6   5   4   3   2   1

First Edition

Contents

1 | Introduction

Many people are finding that skipping rope is the most fun, most convenient, and fastest way to exercise every day. Physical fitness and medical experts agree that jumping 15 minutes a day 5 days a week can result in the kind of heart that keeps you feeling young. Rope jumping also greatly improves coordination and timing needed for other sports and recreation. When we were kids, we jumped for the joy of it; now, as adults, we can enjoy this activity while strengthening the heart and lungs as well as the rest of the body at the same time.

Skipping as exercise requires jumping continuously, with very brief rest breaks. This takes the coordination and stamina to skip about 130 jumps in a row—a minute's worth of rope jumping. By learning to do it correctly and by building your abilities gradually, you can be skipping to fitness within 2 weeks.

This book outlines a 2-week program that will teach you skipping skills and how to use them to attain valuable improvements in your body—no matter who you are. With simple instructions and photographs, you'll learn the basic jump-rope steps, while safely and slowly building your stamina over a 2-week practice period that I will coach you through. Two weeks and you'll be ready to do the Skipout—the basic daily workout you can do almost anywhere, anytime. And you can count on it to provide the heart and lung fitness you need, as well as some terrific total body benefits, including firmer muscle tone.

This is a beginner's book, but anyone who already knows how to jump rope will find all she or he needs to use rope skipping as a primary exercise for the heart. If you already know how to jump rope well, simply review the proper form on page 6, and move right on to the Skipout, page 44.

WHAT CHANGES CAN YOU EXPECT TO SEE?

The good news will greet you in the mirror. For one thing, you'll lose fat overall and gain more muscle definition for a firmer as well as more capable body. Leaner thighs, a more sculpted look to the shoulders, and a flatter stomach are just a few of the physical changes that will make your body look better.

Yet it is the improvements you can't see that make it worth dedicating yourself to "skipping out"—your 20-minute a day, 5-day-a-week Skipout, a fitness workout in which you'll warm up and stretch for 5 minutes, then have fun skipping to a healthy heart.

Exactly what's happening inside your body from this process of continuous, regular exercise is the "miracle" of aerobic or cardiovascular (heart and lung) fitness. Skipping, like running, swimming, and rowing, requires that your heart pump blood to wash every part of your body with oxygen and nutrients. This benefits you even if you do it briefly and sporadically, but when you do it *continuously* and *regularly*, something really wonderful happens to your heart.

The heart, which is really the engine of your body, can become healthier and more efficient not only for your workout but also during your ordinary daily hours. This energy engine will be able to pump as much blood as you need with less effort than before. Your heart becomes more and more able to serve you while working less hard.

Do you see what this efficiency could mean for the long term? If your heart can do just as much work with a minimum of effort, you'll have more energy every day, and perhaps even a longer life, than if you didn't exercise regularly. Some have become concerned these days that strenuous exercise might be detrimental to people who haven't exercised in years. I'd like to emphasize that while this program is beneficial, it is not extreme by any means. Dr. Kenneth Cooper, an aerobic fitness expert, says that skipping rope is an excellent way to achieve cardiovascular fitness.

The prize you're guaranteed by meeting your daily skipping goal is feeling better physically every day. You'll probably begin feeling this improvement after 3 weeks, maybe sooner. The happy paradox is that exercising vigorously actually creates more vigor for you in your other daily activities, and it will help you sleep more soundly at night.

Not only will you be infused with energy and well-being, but also your increased muscle strength and improved anatomical flexibility will make you better prepared for any sudden physical demands or emergencies you might meet in your life. You'll be better able to perform what's necessary with less risk of injuring

YOU'LL LOOK GOOD	YOU'LL FEEL GOOD
• Firmer flesh • Rosy skin tone • Better muscle definition in the shoulders (for more of that wide-shouldered, narrow-hipped body shape) • Leaner, firmer thighs and calves • Flatter stomach • More flexible wrists • Better posture	• Stronger muscles (improved strength especially in the shoulders, arms, legs, and stomach) • Lower resting pulse rate for a more efficient heart • Lighter weight with less fat to carry around • More flexibility in the joints for a reduced chance of injury and of arthritis • More energy overall • Better coordination for sports and recreation

yourself. Even if it's something as simple as hauling down a heavy box from the top shelf of your closet without throwing your back out, it's worth it to devote this small part of your day to your physical well-being.

Because you're staying "still" in the upper body, but flexing the muscles there all the time, skipping rope is virtually an isometric exercise for the upper body—and this means better muscle and skin tone. Jumping rope demands heavy work from the calves, deltoids (shoulder muscles), and forearms, and it is there

---

HOW TO TAKE YOUR PULSE

You can gauge both the caliber of your rope skipping and your heart's improved efficiency by learning to measure your pulse rate while exercising and when at rest. First of all, tomorrow morning right when you wake up but before you get out of bed, reach over for a watch or clock with a second hand, find the point of strongest pulse on your body (either the side of your throat or the inside of your wrist) with your fingers, and count how many pulse beats you can feel in 60 seconds

The best way of gauging your pulse rate during exercise is to count how many times your pulse beats over 10 seconds, then multiply that number by 6 for your rate over the minute. (Of course, anyone over 35 or overweight should check with a doctor before starting any exercise program.) This is your resting pulse rate. Write that number in the corner of your log on page 45. After six months of rope skipping, take your pulse again, on the morning after a rest day. If it is lower than your former resting pulse rate, you know you've improved. Keep in mind, however, that improved fitness does not manifest itself in a lowered resting pulse rate for some people.

If your resting pulse rate does not slow down over time, don't worry. You can make sure you're exercising at a beneficial intensity by measuring your pulse rate during exercise. After a few minutes of skipping, stop and count your exercising pulse rate: it should be a number around 80 percent of 220 minus your age. For example, I am 37, so my aerobic exercise pulse rate should be around $.80 \times 220 - 37$, or 146, a number I derived by subtracting 37 from 220 (for 183), then multiplying 183 by .80.

that you'll experience the most fatigue initially, but the most improved muscle definition and strength eventually. In addition, rope jumping tones the front and back of the thighs (quadriceps and hamstrings) as well as the buttocks, abdominals (stomach muscles), lats and biceps (muscles in the back and in the upper arms), and the lower back (in general the most common area of nonacute injury in adults).

4 STEPS FOR BEGINNERS

Skipping rope is easy. Remember doing it as a kid? What might be more difficult is learning to skip *continuously.* That's what this section is all about: you're going to learn the form that will make it easy to skip 130 or so jumps per minute without stopping. That's all the coordination you need to develop to use rope jumping as your heart's exercise.

Gradually your heart and lungs will become so strong that you won't have to stop as often as every minute to rest. Soon you'll be doing the Skipout: 15 consecutive minutes per day, with 15 seconds of rest between each minute. And right this minute you're going to start on that road to fitness. All physical learning and development is *gradual,* so don't be impatient with yourself.

Know that you *can* learn the simple skills you need; know that you *can* slowly and steadily build the stamina you'll need. This is the first step in the series of instructions that follow which will guide you after 2 weeks to your regular Skipout workout.

Step 1 | KNOW YOU CAN DO IT

Visualize yourself skipping as well as the person pictured on this page. Look at the photograph. It could as well be you in the mirror. Supporting you is the foundation of proper form that enables you to do the Skipout. Read each rule of form, one by one; you'll know them by heart soon enough. Come back to this page as often as you want and read the rules over again.

POINTS OF FORM

1. One hop to every turn of the rope. *Not* 2 jumps, as you used to do as a kid. The first few days of your 2-week practice period program will help you break the 2-jump habit. If you still have trouble jumping only once per rope turn, focus on turning the rope quickly with a crisp snap of the wrists so you create the quick rhythm that brings the single-hop jump with it. Both feet touch the ground when the rope is at the top of its arc, so you're jumping up as the rope is coming down. Land on the balls of your feet, *not* your heels.

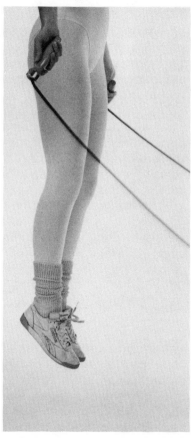

2. *Jump between 1 and 5 inches off the floor.* The lower the hop, the better. Practice this by concentrating on keeping your knees bent only very slightly—no more than a 15-degree angle. If you're jumping too high, you're bending your knees too much. Your knees slightly bent are your shock absorbers; keeping your knees bent as you touch down cushions the force of impact.

DO   **DON'T**

DON'T

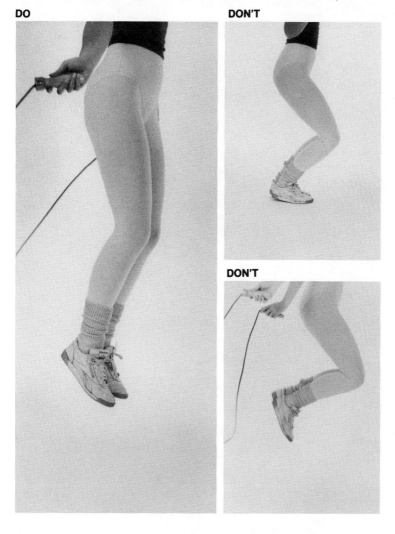

3. *Elbows in, rope handles held waist high.* With your elbows tucked in at your sides, you naturally hold the rope handles waist high about a foot from each side of your waist. Holding the handles any higher constricts your turning of the rope; holding them lower involves too much of an arm-swinging motion, when what you want is to turn the rope with small revolutions from the wrists.

4. Flick your wrists crisply in small circles. This way you'll be turning the rope from your wrists, *not* swinging it with your arms. If you look in the mirror, your upper arms should be stationary. By making tiny circles with your wrists holding the handles, you're making the big revolutions of the rope. To bring the rope over rapidly, the wrists should snap crisply each time the toes bounce.

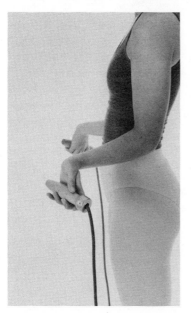

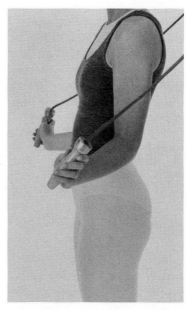

5. Look directly ahead as you skip. This keeps the body aligned. Keeping your eyes leveled in front of you goes a long way toward helping you jump continuously. Don't look at your feet—you'll lose your balance and miss. Looking down makes you step on the rope too often. Keep your balance by keeping your eyes aiming directly ahead of you.

6. Concentrate and focus. By *concentrating* on these points of form, individually at first, then eventually all together, you'll be able to skip continuously and smoothly after you build up some endurance. If at any time you feel fatigued or even just bored, *focus* on a part of your body that's feeling good and performing well. If, for example, your calves feel tired, focus on your wrists: think how tiny a circle you're making with them, revolving the handles of the rope. Or, if your shoulders become tired, focus on how lightly you can hop on the balls of your feet. By concentrating and focusing, you'll find you can actually correct and overcome problems while you're skipping.

7. _Patience is the key._ Skipping rope is one of those odd things that are ludicrously easy once you have learned how but maddeningly evasive as you're trying to learn. Stick with it, day by day. Follow the elementary learning steps and you'll place it all together sooner than you think—with _patience._

Step 2 | PICK A DAY

Decide when you're going to start—any day will do—but be sure to begin on the day you said you would. I'll make beginning easy for you: your first day will take 15 minutes. You can afford 15 minutes, can't you? Mark it on your calendar and look forward to it.

Step 3 | GATHER YOUR EQUIPMENT

This is a fun part of preparation. All you need is a pair of shoes, a clock or watch by which you can count seconds precisely, a place to skip rope on, and, of course, a jump rope.

- _Shoes._ They should be comfortable, flexible, soft-soled, with perhaps a bit more support in the toe area than in the heel. For this reason, so-called aerobic shoes are better than running shoes. Running shoes often have a good deal of support and weight in the heel area—you don't need that. You need shoes that will bend nicely (flexible) and give you a bit of support when you land toward your toes on the balls of your feet—that's the kind of shoes people wear for aerobic dance or exercise classes at the local gym. Soft or rubber-soled shoes provide the flexibility and support you'll need. Wear them around for a while before you start your 2-week practice period, to break them in so they're comfortable.
- _Clock or watch._ It's convenient to skip rope in front of a large wall clock with a second hand—that way you don't have to stop and look at your watch while you're skipping. But since I'll teach you later how to gauge your time by counting your jumps, a digital watch, stopwatch, or basic watch with a second hand will do just fine.

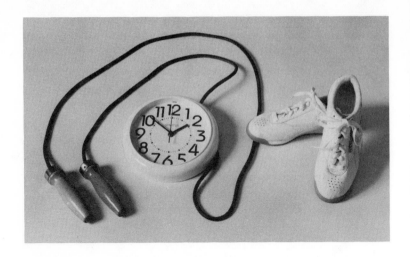

- *Place.* Naturally, you can jump rope almost anywhere—that's one of the reasons it's such a handy exercise. Yet, preferably, you should choose a place to start that has a fairly soft surface. A carpeted or wood floor is best, since both will "give" a little with the weight of your body, thus reducing the impact of force up from the ground through your legs to your knees. A carpet takes a bit of getting used to, because the rope can get stuck on the pile and because your calves must work harder to push off from the soft surface, whereas a wood floor is good right away. An asphalt surface is better than cement. Of course, make sure, if you jump indoors, that the ceiling is high enough (about 15 inches taller than you) to allow for turns of the rope. The minimum floor space you need is 10 by 5 feet.

HOW TO CHOOSE A ROPE

You have your choice among many kinds of ropes now: leather ones with wood handles, plastic ropes with padded handles, even digital ropes that count jumps, and many more. Any will be good for you, so long as it has the following characteristics:

- *Ball bearings in the handles.* The ball bearings keep the rope turning smoothly without too much extra effort from you. This will help keep the rope going consistently so you can concentrate on your jumping form. Ball bearing ropes also last longer.

- *Heavyweight rope material.* This helps you turn the rope smoothly, too, with less effort. I like leather ropes, but a plastic or cotton-fiber rope will do so long as it's weighted.
- *Comfortable handles.* Whether you choose wood, plastic, or foam-padded handles, make sure that they feel and fit right in your hands and that you like the touch of them.
- *The right length.* Obviously this is a very important factor. Find out whether the rope is the right length for you by stepping on the middle of the rope with both feet: if the top of the handles touch your armpits, it fits you. If you have a rope that's too long, tie a loop beneath each handle to make it shorter. If you have to tie a double loop, you should probably get a shorter rope. The rope is the proper length for you if its highest arc passes about a foot over your head as you skip.

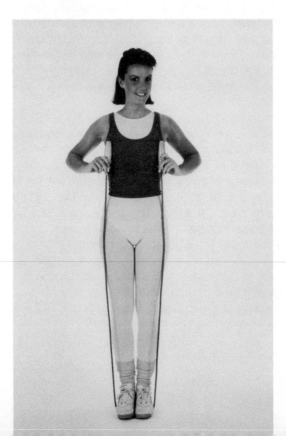

Step 4 | TAKE A HIKE

The more active you've been before starting the program, the better. If you haven't moved around much for a long time, be sure to get some daily exercise for a few weeks before beginning the following 2-week practice period. Jog a little every day, or swim some laps in the local pool. If nothing else, walk vigorously around the block a few times every morning and evening. This will help minimize the muscle soreness you might feel at first and prepare the body better for the exercise ahead so you won't injure yourself by hopping into action too suddenly.

The 2-week practice period workouts on the coming pages will prepare you for the Skipout—the basic workout by which you can use jumping rope as your avenue to building and maintaining a healthy heart. Follow it day by day. If you already know how to skip rope well, you may want to simply review the first 3 days, and begin on Day 4. If you're a beginner, follow it every day—it will teach you the skills you need while building your stamina day by day in the gradual way that is always best for learning safely and well.

If you have difficulty performing what is asked of you on any particular day, no problem. Just repeat the instructions for that day on the following day until you can perform the exercise comfortably, then pick up where you left off. It may take you a little longer that way, but you'll be well prepared for the Skipout.

For days 1 through 3, you have the option of jumping with or without the rope. Try always to use the rope, but if on any day you find you're not getting the hang of it, then do the exercises without the rope. You'll be growing in endurance either way.

One day, believe it, it will simply come to you how easy skipping rope really is. Until the knack comes, keep trying to learn it and trust you will be a rope skipper one day very soon.

Now you're ready to begin. Enjoy yourself. In 2 weeks, you're going to be skipping to a healthy heart!

2 | *The Warm-Up*

The 5-Minute Way to Prepare for the Skipout Every Day

Always warm up before skipping rope—you'll have less risk of injury while you're jumping, and less soreness afterward. Warming up is literally just that. The following exercises will get the blood flowing more readily to every part of your body, heating up the muscle fibers and stretching (lengthening) them as it warms your skin. Warm muscles stretch more easily and better absorb the pounding of your feet against the ground.

Always warm-down after skipping using these exercises or walking until you're breathing normally. Drink plenty of water after exercising and throughout the day.

You'll use these warm-up exercises to start every workout of your 2-week, day-by-day practice program, and you'll begin every Skipout with them later on. So here goes; remember:

• Begin slowly and progress through every movement gradually.
• Stay relaxed and breathe from your diaphragm; exhale fully.
• Hold the positions as illustrated for at least 15 seconds; never bounce.
• Stretch on a soft surface, a rug or a mat.
• Do the exercises in order.
• Never force a position. Go as far as you feel is comfortable— that "burning" sensation is fine, but stop if you feel sharp pain.

Exercise 1 | DANCING IN THE FEET

Begin by "dancing" lightly on the balls of your feet, your weight toward your toes. If you can hear your feet touching the floor, you're bouncing too hard. Pretend you're a boxer getting ready for the ring. Swing your arms around and hop about till you get a light sweat going.

Exercise 2 | SWINGING SHOULDERS

Stand with your feet shoulder width apart, knees slightly bent, and rotate your left arm, first backward 10 times, then forward 10 times. Then rotate your right arm backward 10 times, then forward 10 times.

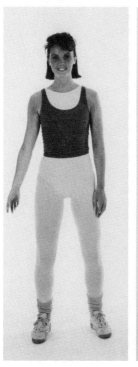

Exercise 3 CALF STRETCHES AND TOE HIGHS

Stand between 2 and 3 feet from the wall, facing it with your knees locked. With your heels flat on the floor, lean in toward the wall, pressing your arms against it at chest height, and hold for 15 seconds. Then stand upright again and rise up and down on your toes 20 times. Repeat the calf stretch again against the wall; then rise up and down on your toes again. Do this complete process once more.

Exercise 4 | THIGH SIGHS

Stand balancing yourself against the wall with one hand. Pull your ankle up until your heel touches your buttocks and your knee is pointing toward the ground. Hold for 10 seconds. Repeat with the other leg.

Exercise 5 | HAMMING IT UP

Stand, legs shoulder width apart, knees locked. Bend at the waist, keeping a flat, straight back, until your fingertips touch the floor (it doesn't matter if you can only reach your socks). Even if you can't put your hands flat on the floor (I certainly can't!), you're still warming the backs of your thighs (hamstrings) by going as far down as you can go comfortably.

Exercise 6 | ANKLE CIRCLES

Rotate your ankle in a circle 10 times counterclockwise, then 10 times clockwise; then rotate your other ankle the same way. Do both these sets of 10 twice on each leg, for 80 ankle circles in all.

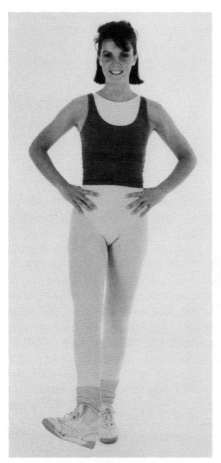

3 | The 2-Week, Day-by-Day Practice Program

DAY 1 | HOP IN PLACE

1. Warm up. Remember to stretch slowly, gradually. Be near a clock or a watch you can use to count the passage of seconds. Be precise.

2. Hop in place: without the rope, bounce on the balls of your feet 10 times, both feet at the same time. Then rest 10 seconds and hop 10 again. Your heels aren't touching the ground—you're jumping up and down toward your toes. Remember to bend your knees no more than 15 degrees as you hop. Keep your eyes looking directly ahead. Do this 10 times: hop 10, rest 10 seconds, hop, rest, and so on, as you would if you were jumping rope.

3. Now, notice how high you're jumping—it's probably too high. Jump this same series of 10 again, this time letting your feet leave the ground no more than 5 inches. You need never jump higher to skip rope. During the 10-second rest periods, remind yourself to concentrate on keeping good posture while you're hopping: back straight, shoulders back, stomach in (as if you were pushing your navel toward your spine with the abdominal muscles).

4. Hop your last series of 10 × 10 jumps (10 at a time followed by 10 seconds of rest) while pointing your elbows into your sides, your hands and forearms at waist level. This is the position in which you will be skipping rope.

DO

DON'T

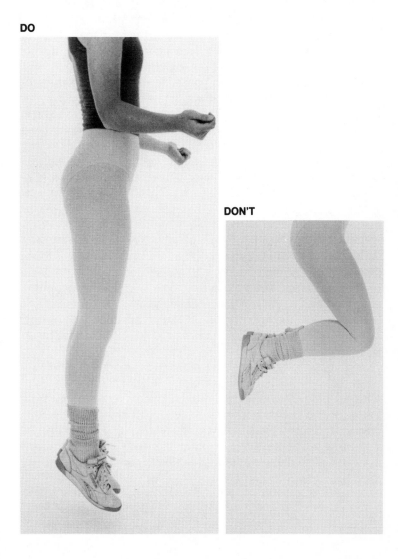

DAY 2 | SWING TEN

1. Warm up.

2. Today, let's add the rope. After you warm up, take hold of both rope handles in one hand and swing the rope in a circle by your side. (Stand well out of the way of Grandma's bone china!) Feel the weight of it; get a sense of its nature. The rope makes its own way around and over without your having to swing it much, doesn't it? This will be true when you're skipping with it, too.

3. Now, tuck your elbow into your side, hand holding the rope handle, forearm jutting out at waist level, and swing the rope again. See how your wrist is capable of sending the rope on its revolutions quite well. In rope jumping, the wrists, not the arms, turn the rope.

4. With these circling motions of your right wrist, send the rope on its circuit by your side 10 times. Then switch hands and do the same thing on your left side, making 10 swings. (If the rope gets tangled, untangle it and start again for 10 in a row.) Do this 10 times in a row on each side.

5. Let's get back to hopping. You're getting your legs (mostly your calves) used to some good work. Hop 20 in a row today, then rest 10 seconds and hop 20 again, and so on for a series of 10. Remember: keep elbows in, eyes level ahead, good posture; land on the balls of your feet, knees slightly bent.

6. Now swing the rope again: 10 times on each side without stopping, for a series of 5 on each side. Untangle your rope before putting it away.

7. Hop 10 × 10 again this time with only 5 seconds rest between each set, then you're done for the day. Tonight might be the night for a hot bath. With legs outstretched in the tub, bend forward at the waist and pull your toes toward you for a few good stretches, then extend them away from you, alternating. A good soak in hot water or a whirlpool bath is a nice thing to do for your legs, and it will minimize muscle soreness for tomorrow.

DAY 3 | REST AND REVIEW

Just do your warm-up exercises today, emphasizing the slowness of your stretching. Try to stretch farther today, but stop short of pain, of course. Anytime you feel sharp pain, stop before you try again. It is natural to feel a diffuse, dull ache at this point, even if you're not brand-new to exercise. Understand that this type of soreness is a sign that your muscles are learning something new: they're growing stronger, building stamina, just as your heart and lungs are beginning to increase their endurance, too. Learn to recognize this type of warm ache, which is really just fatigue, as a good sign—it means your strength is improving. But give yourself a break, too, and maybe even another hot bath. The soreness will become less frequent, and after a few weeks of the Skipout you'll feel little to none.

Because your weight hits the ground through your feet after every jump, skipping rope can put great stress on the lower legs, both front and back. As your calves develop strength, the soreness there will subside over time. Too much stress on the front of the lower leg sometimes causes lower leg pain or even "shin splints," so if you ever feel sharp pain there, take a rest from jumping till it goes away. Meanwhile, to fortify your legs to accommodate that extra stress, repeat the calf stretches and toe highs part of your warm-up several times a day and do the toe-extension exercise mentioned for Day 2 whenever you think of it: in a sitting position, pull your toes toward you with your hands, then point your toes away from you, repeating in alternate fashion like this at least 10 times.

While you're soaking in the tub, review page 6 for proper form. Tomorrow you're going to become a rope skipper.

DAY 4 | SKIP ROPE

1. Warm up.
2. Hop in place, 10 × 10, resting 5 seconds between each set of 10. Concentrate on proper form (page 6).
3. Swing where you are (as you did on Day 2), 10 × 5, both sides.
4. Now, letting the rope lie flaccid behind you, hold a handle in each hand and hop in place, 20 × 10, resting 10 seconds between each set. Remember, you're not turning the rope over your head yet—you're still getting the feel of it. Revolve your wrists as you're hopping, if you like, but don't turn the rope yet.

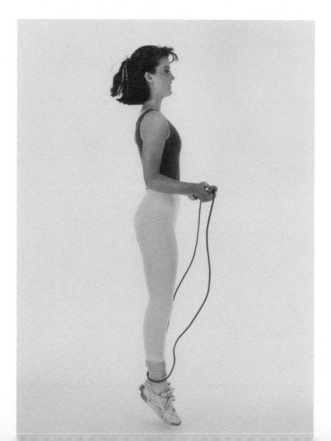

5. OK, let's try a few. You know how to skip rope—you did it as a kid—jump rope now. Whoops! What happened! Form flew out the window, right? You leaped 4 feet into the air on every jump and got tired after 3 turns. Or you jumped as if you were trying to scale a fence, and landed right on the rope.

That's all right. There's a good bit of tripping in skipping. Always was, always will be. What you've got to do is skip as best you can today—for 5 full minutes. I don't care if you step on the rope 500 times, and neither should you. Today is the day you exercise a strength in your head: it's called patience.

6. The 5 minutes are up. Are you still with us? Tear your hair out yet? Good, still a few left. Now repeat step 4 without turning the rope. Doing that fine, are you? Well, that's no different from skipping rope. Don't believe me? The difference is in your head. Review page 6: elbows in, eyes level ahead, knees only slightly bent, hopping no more than 5 inches off the floor. You can do it with the rope, too—and that's exactly what you're going to do from now on.

7. But first, let's build some more stamina today. Put the rope aside, then hop in place, 25 × 10, with 10 seconds rest between each set of 25.

DAY 5 | HOP TWO

1. Warm up.
2. Hop in place, without the rope, 20 × 10, resting 5 seconds between each set of 20.
3. Swing 5: Alternating arms, swing the rope 10 × 5, each arm.
4. Simply relax and skip rope for about a minute, stopping and starting up again as needed. Remember, you're practicing patience as much as anything else today. Breathe deeply, exhale fully throughout, but make a special point of concentrating on your breathing every time you miss and as you're arranging the rope again to begin anew.
5. Rest, standing in place for a full minute while you review the rules (proper form) on page 6.
6. Hop in place, paying special attention to jumping no higher than 5 inches off the ground—2 inches is preferable. In fact, try hopping off the balls of your feet just 2 inches up each time, barely off the floor. Keep your eyes level ahead as you're doing this, however. Practice this low hop in front of a full-length mirror a few times, if you can, just to get the feel of how low you should be jumping, or ask a friend to tell you when it looks as though your jump is no more than 2 inches.
7. Now hop in place 20 × 10, concentrating on hop height, keeping eyes level ahead. During your 10-second rest periods, think of all the other elements in proper form and practice them: good posture, stomach in, knees only slightly bent. Then go back to concentrating on keeping your eyes straight ahead and your jump low for the next 20 hops, and so on. Remember to hold your elbows in at your sides.
8. Skip rope again for 5 minutes as best you can, this time concentrating on keeping your eyes level ahead of you and keeping your hop very low, try for 1 or 2 inches high. Your elbows are resting at your sides; your wrists are turning the rope, not your arms. It doesn't matter how many times you miss or step on the rope. Just make sure not to rest longer than 10 seconds before starting up again.

9. Finish off with a precise counting round of hopping in place, 30 × 10, without the rope, if you like. Exactly count each 30 jumps, using perfect form as described on page 6, and spend your 10-second recovery periods enjoying how your deep breathing and full exhaling relax and rest you. Then hop 30 more, rest, hop, and so on, until you've hopped a series of 10 30-jump sections, a total of 300 hops.

1. Warm up.

2. Hop in place (or skip rope), 30 × 10, with 10-second rest breaks, concentrating on rules of form, page 6.

3. Skip rope for 5 minutes as well as you can: no pauses longer than 10 seconds, no swearing (breathe in and exhale fully once for every expletive you might have uttered). This time concentrate on making little circles with your wrists—these are the small circles that grow into the big revolutions of the rope. With them, making the rope turn into a circle is almost as easy as making circles by dropping a pebble into a pond. Very little effort is needed on your part. Your revolving wrists flick the rope over, and the weight of the rope plus another little flicker of wrist motion brings the rope down in front of you and around under your feet and on over your head again. *Don't swing the rope with your arms.* Concentrate on sending the rope around with your wrist circles, as if you were cranking the handle inside a car door to open the window.

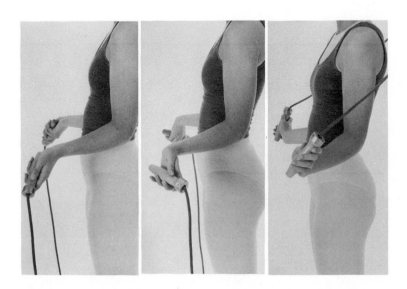

During your rest periods, remind yourself to keep your eyes level and your hop low. But concentrate on those smooth flicks of your wrists while you're skipping. It's a slight motion. Stop and review it by swinging 10 when you need to (see Day 2).

4. Hop in place (or skip rope), this time resting only 5 seconds between 20-jump sets in your series of 10. Keep those elbows perched in at your sides.

5. Rest 60 seconds and think about that delicious bath that awaits you tonight and the day off you've earned tomorrow.

6. Hop in place (or skip rope), 10 × 10, resting only 5 seconds between every 10 jumps. Remind yourself of the rules of form (page 6) and concentrate on them individually, a different rule for every set of 10.

7. Repeat steps 5 and 6, then congratulate yourself.

DAY 7 | DAY OFF

You should probably still do 10 minutes of stretching/warm-up exercises today, but "skip" 'em if you want the whole day off.

DAY 8 | ROPE YOUR RHYTHM

1. Warm up for a full 10 minutes, or more if you feel like it.
2. Hop in place (or skip rope), 20 × 10, with 5-second recovery periods, using each set to concentrate on a point of form. Afterward, list those you still have trouble with.
3. Skip rope as continuously as you can for 5 minutes, concentrating on clearing the rope and not missing. Rest no more than 10 seconds between efforts. Breathe; don't be discouraged; practice your patience. Keep in mind:

   You skip once only for every turn of the rope.

   You're jumping with both feet at once, on the balls of your feet.

   The rope hits the floor right before you hop; when you hear your feet hit, the rope is at the top.

   Rope jumping has a rhythm and a smoothness.

   Listen for your own pace and follow the rhythm of it, not the rope's rhythm.

4. Rest 60 seconds.
5. Hop in place (or skip rope), 50 × 5, resting 15 seconds between each set of 50.
6. Use your recovery period now to go put on some music. Pick something lively that you like a lot.
7. Skip for 5 minutes as you did in step 3. Don't try to jump rope to the rhythm of the music; simply let the music relax you so you can enjoy the rhythm of your rope jumping as if it had its own particular sound that it makes in your head. You'll find it does.

DAY 9 | COUNTING TIME

1. Warm up.

2. Hop in place (or skip rope), 50 × 2, resting for 15 seconds exactly between the 2 sets of 50.

3. Rest 60 seconds and review form on page 6. If you've identified a particular problem you have (check that list you made yesterday) that might be causing you to miss too often, concentrate on correcting it during the following. (Remember: if you're going by the form on page 6 but still stepping on the rope too often, you're hopping too late. Your feet should touch the ground when the rope is at the top of the arch, so that you're jumping up as the rope is coming down.)

4. Now, relax and skip rope for 10 minutes as continuously as you can. You may rest 15 seconds for every 60-second rope skipping period you accomplish, but do not stop during each minute's rope jumping for more than 5 seconds after you miss. Even if you step on the rope, just go right on. Gather yourself together within 5 seconds and proceed. Relax, be patient. If you're missing too often, you might be looking down at your feet. Remember to keep your eyes aimed straight ahead.

5. Very good. Now let's try to count how many skips you can do in a minute. Skip in front of a wall clock with a big second hand today, or ask a friend to time each 60-second period for you, while you concentrate on counting. Or do 130 skips and check your wristwatch to see how close to a minute you are. (Eventually, the more skips per minute you can do, the more fat you burn. But for now, consistency is the key.) When you learn how many jumps a minute's worth is for you, you'll be able to skip anywhere, which will make your Skipout a very convenient form of exercise.

Now, skip 1 minute 5 times, resting no more than 15 seconds between every 60-second period. Don't worry if you miss; just proceed as you did in step 4 and keep counting till a minute is up. Have a pencil and paper handy so that during each 15-second rest period between every minute you can write down how many jumps you accomplished for the minute.

6. Stop. Add the 5 numbers together and divide the sum by 5. The answer is the average number of jumps you're presently able

to do in 1 minute. It should be at least 100, but it's OK if it's not; you'll become consistent with more practice. Whatever the number is, use it for the next few days as your measure of a minute's worth of skipping so you won't have to look at a clock for a while and you'll be able to concentrate on polishing your form.

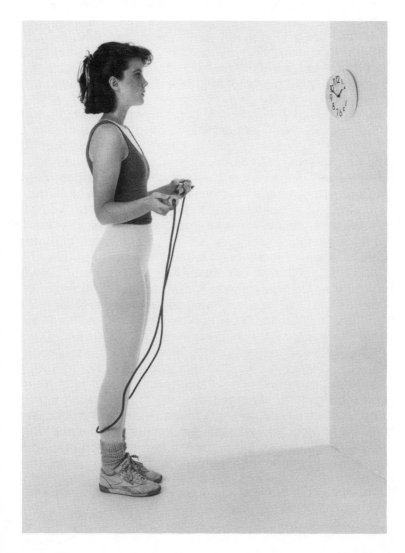

DAY 10 | TROUBLE SHOOTING

Tomorrow is your day off, so today let's put it all together and find out what areas you need to concentrate on the day after tomorrow so you'll truly be ready to do the Skipout after these 2 weeks come to an end.

1. Warm up.

2. Skip rope, 1 minute × 5, counting out each minute's worth, using the average number you found yesterday. Today, try to skip in front of a full-length mirror and a wall clock or with a friend who can watch you to see if you're employing all the points of form that help you jump continuously. Remember to rest no more than 15 seconds between each minute's worth of jumping.

3. After a 60-second rest, spend another 5 minutes or so skipping rope, but this time don't count—concentrate on continuous skipping instead. And every time you miss, stop and try to notice what you were doing at the moment you missed and what made you step on the rope. Were you looking down and did you get off balance? Keeping your eyes level and looking directly ahead of you will correct this problem. During your next effort at continuous skipping, concentrate on keeping your eyes level ahead.

Next time you miss, ask yourself the same questions. Were you jumping too high with your knees bent too much before you landed on the rope? If so, concentrate next time on keeping your legs fairly straight and hopping no higher than 5 inches off the ground; the lower you hop, the better.

Take as much time as you need between efforts at continuous skipping to figure out a problem of form to focus on. If you or your friend or the mirror can't identify the specific thing you're doing wrong that's making you miss, refer to page 6 and proceed through every point of form listed there. You're bound to correct your particular problem through the process of elimination. This may take longer than 5 minutes, but take the time today—the practice will serve you well later, and tomorrow you can take the day off.

4. Now that you're finished troubleshooting, build your stamina. You may have been missing simply out of fatigue, so increasing your endurance will eventually solve that problem. Just keep going

and don't get discouraged. Great improvements seem to happen all at once, but really they're the product of slow, steady development over time. Jump rope 5 minutes, skipping as continuously as you can for each full minute, resting exactly 15 seconds between every 60 seconds. Use either the clock or the number of jumps per minute you know you do, whichever is more comfortable for you, in order to count each minute's worth.

| **DAY 11** | RELAX |

Day off, and well deserved too!

Do just your stretching exercises after a hot bath tonight before you go to bed.

| **DAY 12** | BUILDING ENDURANCE |

1. Warm up.
2. The day before yesterday, perhaps you were missing, not because of any special problem in your form, but just because you were tired. That's why days like today are especially important to prepare you for the Skipout. The more diligently you perform today's workout, the less tired you'll become 3 days from now, on your first day of the Skipout.

Skip rope 1 minute × 5, using the clock if possible so you don't have to count and you can concentrate on form. Rest 30 seconds between each minute and figure out what point of form you need to focus on for the next minute's worth of continuous skipping. Refer to what you found out on Day 10.
3. Rest 60 seconds. Then skip rope, 25 jumps × 10, resting 5 seconds between each set of 25. Concentrate on being continuous and relaxed. Don't forget to breathe smoothly and exhale fully; get a rhythm going.
4. Rest 60 seconds. Then skip rope, 50 jumps × 5, resting 5 seconds between each set as you did in step 3.
5. Rest 60 seconds. Then skip rope your minute's worth (at least 100 jumps) twice, resting only 5 seconds between. This might be taxing, but do your best—it's almost over.
6. Rest 60 seconds. Finally, finish off by jumping rope, 25 jumps × 10, resting 5 seconds between each set of 25. Focus on getting 25 exactly without missing—you can do it.
7. Go right to your warm-up exercises and use them to warm down. You've done well. The Skipout will be easier than today was!

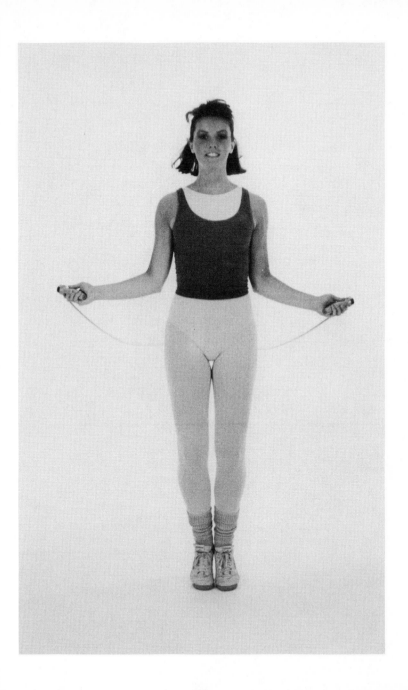

Today will be a fairly light day, a day for review and keen observation to identify any areas in which you need practice to perfect your rope jumping skill.

1. Warm up.

2. Jump rope for 5 minutes, resting for 15 seconds between each minute. Put on some music for this and relax, concentrating on regular, smooth breathing. When you miss, proceed smoothly on as if nothing happened, so that you're jumping for a full minute each minute if you can.

3. How did you do? Now's the time to analyze, while you recover for 60 seconds. If missing is keeping you from getting into the rhythm of pleasurable rope jumping, let's practice each of the points of form.

Jump rope again as you did in step 2, 1 minute × 5, 15 seconds of rest, this time choosing the 5 points of form you've found to be most helpful to your skipping continuously and focusing on one of them for each minute you jump. For example, how about rule 3 on page 8: think elbows in, hands at waist level out to your sides turning little circles with the rope while you skip for your first full minute. For the second minute concentrate on keeping your eyes level ahead; and so on through the list.

4. While you rest now for 60 seconds, ask yourself: was any point of form more difficult to perform than the others? If so, focus on that point for this entire last 5-minute session. Skip rope 1 minute × 5, resting only 5 seconds between each minute this time.

DAY 14 | GET READY FOR THE SKIPOUT

1. Warm up.
2. The Skipout Run-through: simply jump rope 15 minutes, resting 30 seconds between each minute (a longer rest than the Skipout needs). Let's break the 15 minutes into 3 segments and use each for good purpose.

   A. Relax, be patient, enjoy yourself. Spend the first 5 minutes just doing the best you can, trying for continuity and enjoyment in the activity. Play some music.

   B. Practice the form that helps you. Use the second 5 minutes to focus on proper form, giving special attention to the particular points of form that you've found help you skip most continuously. During the 30-second rest periods between minutes, breathe smoothly from the diaphragm; exhale fully.

   C. Measure your minute's worth. For your last 5 minutes, watch the clock and count how many jumps you accomplish in each 1-minute set, then write the numbers down during your rest periods.
3. Finally, add the 5 numbers and divide by 5 for the average number of jumps you're doing now in a 60-second period. I'll bet it's a bigger number than your first average from Day 9. If it isn't yet, it will be after you're well into your Skipout.
4. Write your new number average in the space provided in your log, page 45. This is the number you'll be using for the first few weeks of the Skipout, so you won't have to watch the clock too much and you can focus on keeping up your form and enjoying yourself.

Now you're ready to begin the Skipout. Why not start tomorrow—you can take your day off the day after that.

4 | *The Skipout*

The Skipout is basically 15 minutes' worth of jumping rope with 15 seconds of rest after each minute (if you need it), 5 days a week. You pick the days; the best coaching advice is to choose the days beforehand and stick to your schedule. This will give you satisfaction and a sense of accomplishment, which you deserve, and which will help you proceed even on the days you're not feeling enthusiastic.

When you become ready for some variety in your workouts, go to page 50 and try the variations described there. They will offer you room for advancement as well as renewed freshness in your adventure of skipping toward a healthy heart.

Following is a week's worth (your first week) of the Skipout, to begin right after you finish your 2-week practice period. After this first week, use your log, beginning on page 47 to note your progress during the weeks thereafter.

And here's another tip from your coach: no one is ever going to be perfectly consistent. Every athlete in training for a sport or in training for life takes time off once in a while, maybe even a long time. Even if you come to a point in your life in which your "break" seems to last for weeks or even months, remember to keep this book in a safe place where you can find it when you're ready again. Then begin again; start with the 2-week practice period, and proceed on to the Skipout. Life is a series of beginnings, and you can always start over.

Don't forget: warm up before, warm down after, and drink lots of water all day long.

THE SKIPOUT: A Week's Worth to Get You Hopping

My resting pulse rate is: _____ beats per minute on _____
(month) (day) (year)

I skip an average of: _____ jumps per minute

	This is how I feel about today:
DAY 1: 1. Warm up (see page 15) 2. Jump rope: 15 minutes, rest 15 seconds after each minute (the Skipout) *KEEP IN MIND:* Be patient with yourself. When you miss before a minute is over, just pick up and go on as if nothing happened. Skipping continuously is not jumping perfectly. You don't have to be perfect. Simply proceed with your rope jumping patiently, picking up the count where you left off.	
DAY 2: Rest day.	
DAY 3: 1. Warm up 2. Do the Skipout (same as Day 1) *REVIEW IN YOUR MIND* all the points of form listed on page 00, concentrating on one or another during each minute you jump.	

DAY 4:
1. Warm up
2. Skipout

REMEMBER TO ENJOY YOURSELF.
Put on some music to relax by, but
don't jump *to* the music. Listen
instead to your own pace. Fall into
the rhythm of the rope.

DAY 5:
Rest day.

DAY 6:
1. Warm up
2. Skipout

ASK YOURSELF: Am I aiming my
eyes directly ahead as I jump? Are
my elbows in, hands no higher or
lower than waist level? Am I keeping
my hop low, knees bent at about a
15-degree angle, landing on the
balls of my feet?

DAY 7:
1. Warm up
2. Skipout

RELAX. Skipping rope is easy. Try
not to be hard on yourself, and don't
be frustrated when you step on the
rope. If you find you're missing from
fatigue, take 30-second rest periods
today. You may need more time to
work up to the 15-second recovery
period routine.

5 | *Your Log*

This is your log. Use it to feel proud of yourself as you chart your progress. Next to *Minutes*, log the number of minutes you skipped rope; beside *Skips*, jot down the average number of skips you jumped in 1 minute's time. Write what you feel in your comments: note any aspect you'd like to improve upon next time; if you felt good, try to identify what you were able to do that made you successful at skipping continuously. (Before you begin, make photocopies of these 2 pages so you can keep a log for many months to come.) See example below.

Date:	Minutes:	Skips:
Comments:		

Date:	Minutes:	Skips:
Comments:		

Date:	Minutes:	Skips:
Comments:		

Date:	Minutes:	Skips:
Comments:		

Date:	Minutes:	Skips:
Comments:		

Date:	Minutes:	Skips:
Comments:		

Date:	Minutes:	Skips:
Comments:		

Date:	Minutes:	Skips:
Comments:		

Date:	Minutes:	Skips:
Comments:		

6 | *Variations and Advancement*

Variation #1 | THE TWO-STEP

The 2-step is a variation in your footwork while jumping rope that can provide not only something new to refresh your enthusiasm but also a way to actually rest your legs. Up till now, you've been jumping rope by hopping with both feet simultaneously. Now I want you to try hopping with just one foot at a time. Sound impossible? It's actually very easy. Yet, just as in skipping rope at the beginning, you may have to start over and use the 2-week practice period in which to learn the coordination of it.

Go back to page 22 and begin on Day 1, but instead of doing hopping practice on both feet, alternate your feet as you hop: first jump up on the right foot, then jump on the left foot, and so on, back and forth, through the exercise. Believe me, this will work when you're skipping rope. The rope will pass under one foot, then the other, in the wink of an eye, and you'll be skipping as smoothly—even perhaps more so—as you were with both feet hopping at the same time.

It's almost a shuffling motion your feet make—it looks like running gently in place; the toes will angle out to the side slightly as the rope scoops the air beneath them. Go through the entire 2-week practice cycle again if you need to in order to learn this well, then substitute this step whenever you want in your Skipout.

As an example, for the 2-Step Skipout, hop with both feet for the first minute, then hop the 2-step for the next minute, alternating between them for the rest of the 15 minutes. Or alternate even during each minute, 10 skips with both feet, 10 using the 2-step, 10 with both feet, and so forth. When you master the 2-step, you'll find it to be a welcome relief—even restful—during your Skipout.

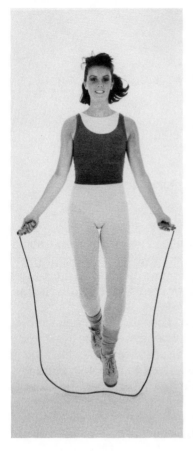
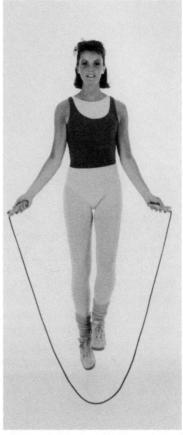

  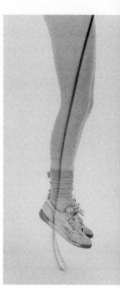

FRED AND GINGER

Remember Fred Astaire and Ginger Rogers? Well, I do. . . . Anyway, in those 1940s movies they danced their way through, sometimes they'd waltz slowly, then break into some quick tapping and twirls. I'm not suggesting you lasso your partner with a rope, but I am encouraging you to try a change of pace. In sports language, it's called *intervals*.

Using your standard Skipout, you can vary your rope jumping pace—and derive some wonderful benefits from it. Try skipping your first minute of Skipout at your usual pace, but for the second minute, skip as fast as you can—can you do 150 skips in a minute? Then for the third minute, skip a bit slower than you're used to; skip fast again for the fourth, and so on.

The benefits? Your usual pace will seem easier than usual. If 130 per minute was your original Skipout pace, several sessions

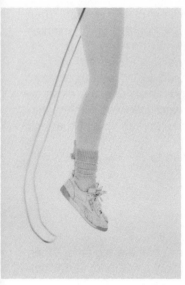

of intervals at 150 will eventually make 150 your comfortable, normal pace, and 175 will become more of a "sprint." The more skips you can consistently do in a minute, the better trained your heart will be—and the more fat you will burn.

Advancement 1: THE JUNIOR OLYMPICS

Well, not really, but still, if you want to advance to a higher level of aerobic fitness, the way to do it is to skip even more continuously than you have in the standard Skipout. You do this by skipping faster than you have been—the more jumps you skip in a minute, the better the workout—or by cutting out the rest breaks as much as you can.

Remember to progress slowly, gradually. Start by trying this: do the Skipout, but this time jump continuously for 2 minutes instead of 1, then rest 30 seconds instead of 15 seconds. Then skip 1 minute, rest 15 seconds. Jump your fourth and fifth minutes consecutively without a rest break between, then rest 15 seconds, and skip the sixth minute, followed by a 15-second rest; the seventh and eighth and ninth minutes consecutively, rest 30 seconds; skip the tenth, followed by 15 seconds' rest; skip the eleventh and twelfth, resting 15 seconds afterward; follow up with the thirteenth, fourteenth, and fifteenth minutes, broken up as usual with 15-second breaks.

Not tired yet? Then you can proceed to...

Advancement 2: THE TRIALS

Every athlete has to win her or his chance at the big time. When you can work "The Junior Olympics" into your Skipout fairly comfortably a couple of times a week, try this:

Skip 5 minutes without stopping, then rest 60 seconds; skip another 5 continuous minutes, rest 60 seconds; skip your last third of the workout as you did the first two-thirds.

Advancement 3: OLYMPIC GOLD

So you think you're Joan Benoit or Edwin Moses, do you? Could be. If you've managed "The Trials" two or three times a week, try tossing this bombshell into your Skipout:

Skip rope continuously for 15 minutes.

I didn't name this with Olympiad terms for nothing. Even world-class athletes in terrific aerobic shape might have difficulty doing this advanced form of Skipout in the beginning; they would have to perfect their rope skipping technique first. But it's one of the best aerobic workouts in the world, as taxing as 15 continuous minutes of running, rowing, swimming, or cross-country skiing.

But, after all, there's a heart of gold at the end.

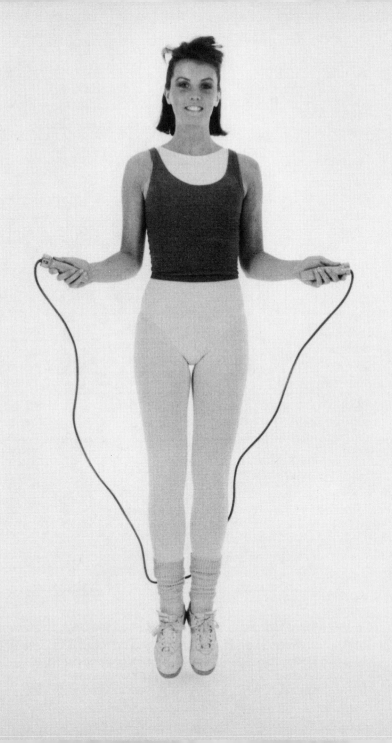

CANDACE LYLE HOGAN is the coauthor of *Diana Nyad's Basic Training for Women* and is the managing editor of *The Runner* magazine. She has been an avid rope-skipper since 1976.